A Bunch o-

Written by Paulin

Illustrated by Elaine Nipper

To Rachel
with love
Elaine Nipper

Dear Rach
love,
Pauline Trav

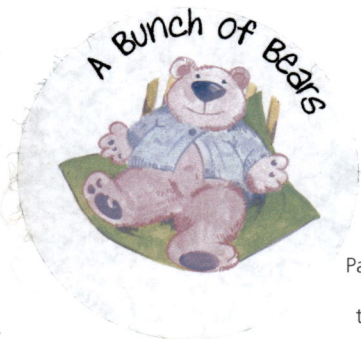

First published by Elaine Nipper in the United Kingdom 2011

ISBN 978-0-9569939-0-8

For further details about Pauline Travers as a visiting author
please contact her via e-mail at paulinetraversat23@aol.com.

www.elainenipper.co.uk

A Bear for Baby

You've a new baby brother."
Daddy said to Faye.
He'll be coming home with mummy,
later on today."

Can I play with him?" she asked.
Will he want to share my toys?"
No, he'll just need sleep and feeding
and he'll make a lot of noise!"

Will he like my dolls or lego?
Will he want to watch T.V?"
No, he'll just snuggle down with mummy,
And cuddle you and me."

"I'd like to give him something,
something special, he will care.
I know what, daddy...
I'll give him my best bear!"

She fetched her well worn teddy,
And sat him in the chair.
A loving gift for baby,
Faye's treasured teddy bear.

After Goldilocks

The locks were changed,
They cut new keys,
And locked the windows,
If you please.
They bought a guard dog from a farm,
Installed a fancy burglar alarm.
The garden gate was built up high
And forest folk, they wondered why?
"It's because of Goldilocks," they said,

"We will feel safer in our beds."
Father bear was well prepared
As baby bear had been so scared.
Mother's porridge was now just right.
She didn't want another fright.
Baby's chair was sent away
To be repaired by next Friday.
And when the bears sat down for tea
They watched for her... on CCTV!

Barbaric Barbers

Brown bear popped to the barbers
and asked for a little trim.
"Would you like a cool cut this morning?"
The barber asked with a grin.

"I think I'm quite a cool bear."
Said the bear feeling rather pleased.
The barber got his clippers out
And the fur he trimmed with ease.

The brown fur fell down softly,
covering the floor like a rug.
The barber chatted casually,
And gave the bear tea in a mug.

Bear looked into the mirror
to admire his new style of hair.
And cool he certainly was going to be.
As now hairless, was totally bare!

Belonging

He's watching me with just one eye,
Perched on a shelf way up high.
He knows my thoughts, my highs and lows.
My moods and laughter and all that goes
With being the bear who belongs.

He's met my friends; been out to tea.
Cuddled me when I've hurt my knee.
Snuggles in bed to keep me warm.
Shared my fears in a nasty storm.
He knows he's a bear who belongs.

He's very brave; he even fights.
He batters my brother with all of his might!
He hides my face when it's full of tears.
His delicate paws rub off grubby smears
From the face of the child who belongs.

Funny Old Bear

Fluffy, furry, soft...not he!
He's bald and scratchy as can be.
He's lost his fur from too much love,
Cuddled, squeezed and tossed above
The heads of children having fun.
(He's got a few hairs on his tum!)
Stuffing's seeping here and there,
But old bear doesn't seem to care.
Paws are patched up, nose as well.
He finds it very difficult to smell.
Legs still move, arms can hug,
He likes to snooze down on the rug.
Ears are floppy, eyes still bold.
Well, that's just part of being old.

Save the Bears

We're bears that are hungry,
We're bears, big and strong,
We're bears with warm coats
That we always keep on.

Deep in the forest where berries are plenty,
We dine each day, so we're never empty.
Although we are large, we can travel at speed.
Remember that, hunter. Listen, take heed!

Yes:
We're bears that are hungry,
We're bears, big and strong,
We're bears with warm coats
That we always keep on.

For years you have sought us for meat and our fur,
But have you thought, did it not occur?
That the meat on our bodies belongs to us,
And remember it's our fur, so don't make a fuss!

SO:
We're bears that are hungry,
We're bears, big and strong,
We're bears with warm coats
That we always keep on.

For years you kept us for crowds to delight,
To dance and to prance from dawn until night.
But we're strictly not dancing for you any more,
We won't sit and beg and we won't wave a paw.

Oh yes!
We're bears that are hungry,
We're bears, big and strong,
We're bears with warm coats
That we always keep on.

Don't tempt us with money or large jars of honey,
Or caves with a clean concrete floor.
Don't tempt us with fame in the cage at the zoo.
For watching sad bears seems to be quite a coo.

Remember:
We're bears that are hungry,
We're bears, big and strong,
We're bears with warm coats
That we always keep on.

And please help our cousins there out in the snow.
Polars need ice and a cold wind to blow.
But what are you doing? You're melting their land.
Just cool it and show you can give them a hand.

Yeah man!
We're bears that are hungry,
We're bears, big and strong,
We're bears with warm coats
That we always keep on.

The bear you can keep is cuddly and game,
Theodore Roosevelt gave Teddy his name.
Out hunting one day he did not want to shoot
A helpless black bear tied to a tree root.

The bear said:
I'm a bear that is hungry,
A bear, big and strong,
I've got a warm coat
That I always keep on.

And from that day to this you love teddy bears.
You cuddle and pet them and sit them on chairs.
But will you remember the real bears out there?
Go on, save the species. Show them you care!

WE ARE WORTH IT!
We're bears that are hungry,
We're bears, big and strong,
We're bears with warm coats
That we always keep on.
GRRRRRRRRRRRRRRR!

Grizzly

Does a Grizzly bear grizzle when he's hunting for his food?
Does he really get so grumpy when he's in a bad mood?
With his thick glossy coat and his handsome face,
To moan about his looks would be a terrible disgrace.

Does he grumble at his cubs when they roll around the floor?
Does he growl and try to smack them with his huge great paw?
When his cave is in a mess and the snow begins to fall,
Does he have a temper tantrum, stamp his feet and start to bawl?

No, he's really not bad natured as his name might just suggest,
In fact, he's quite a funny bear, a proper little pest.
And when he settles down for his long winter sleep,
He's a gentle and contented bear, breathing soft and deep.

Lost

Little brother held him tight,
comforting, soft and warm.
A loved teddy bear,
Patched and balding.

But then it happened!
The parade passed by,
The crowd cheered and jostled,
Everyone waved and shouted.

That's when teddy was lost?
Dropped in the excitement.
Left to fight his own way
Through the tangle of legs.

"Where's my teddy?"
Little brother cried out in panic.
"He's gone, he's lost!"
Tears streamed down his face.

A stranger heard the cry,
looked round and scanned the floor
to save the poor bear,
drowning in the crowd.

"Is this yours?"
"Oh, yes," my brother said;
gulping back the sobs,
cradling teddy in his arms again.

Once upon a Teddy Bear

Once upon a time there was a brave teddy bear,
Who was bought in a toy shop, boxed then and there.
Taken to a post office and sent far away
To a little boy in London for his fifth birthday.

The journey was a long one, full of dread and fear,
The darkness was quite frightening and he shed a little tear.
Then he heard a doorbell ringing and a little boy's cry.
Was this the end of teddy's life, was he going to die?

The box began to shake, as it was gaily ripped apart,
A little hand grabbed him and gave him quite a start!
Then softly, gently, quietly, he was stroked and held quite tight.
So happily ever after, teddy's life looks bright.

Sticky Bear

Too much, too much, too much honey.
His tummy's round and very gummy.
His paws are sticky, his nose is too.
In fact he's covered all over in goo!

Too much, too much, too much honey.
Teddy bear thinks it's far too yummy.
He's stuck his head into the jar.
He is the stickiest bear by far.

Too much, too much, too much honey,
His owner doesn't think it's funny.
On finding this disgusting scene,
She dumps him in the washing machine!

Teddy Bears' Disastrous Picnic.

If you go down to the woods today,
You'll never believe your eyes,
For the teddies are in fancy dress,
Fairies, clowns, pirates and spies.

They've rolled in the honey and sat in the jelly,
Each little bear looks dirty and smelly.
The drinks are all spilt, sandwiches squashed,
Every picnic blanket needs to be washed.

They've got themselves in a terrible state!
But here come their mothers looking quite ira
"You naughty bears, this mess is bad.
It's such a disgrace, you've made us mad!"

The teddies are sad and they quiver with fear.
(Some get a little cuff behind the ear.)
So back home to bed, they are marched away.
That's the end of their picnic for today.

Teddy's Diet

Said teddy Tim to teddy Tom,
"My tummy's round, there's something wrong!"
Teddy Tom felt Tim's round tummy.
"Have you eaten lots of honey?"

"Just two jars of honey sweet,
Now I can't even see my feet!
I'll have to do a teddy diet,
Don't tell a soul, please keep it quiet."

So teddy Tim cut down on honey,
And saved himself a lot of money.
One month later said Tom to Tim.
"We'll change your name to Teddy Slim!"

zoo Bear

Polar, polar, polar bear,
Why do you swing your head and stare?
Is it the concrete pool so small,
That is not like your freezing seas at all?
Is it the new painted wall so bright
That reminds you of snow, deep and white?

Polar, polar, polar bear,
Why do you swing your head and stare?
Is it the fish from the zoo keeper's pail?
Do you miss the haunting song of the whale?
Are you tired of the faces that stare at you,
Or bored with just having nothing to do?

Polar, polar, polar bear,
Why do you swing your head and stare?

Barney Bear

The suitcase was packed and it stood by the door,
Barney bear watched from his seat on the floor.
His family bustled and hurried around,
He felt more worried down there on the ground.

Where were they going and would they be long?
He was sure he would miss them; he'd have to be strong.
He had his best clothes on, his scarf and his hat.
But would they forget him, as he sat on the mat?

Then they were gone and the door was shut tight.
His little head drooped, would he be all right?
Then like an explosion, Jack came through the door!
"I've got him, mummy, he's here on the floor."

Swept up in Jack's arms, his teddy heart' glowed,
And he smiled his bear smile - I don't think it showed.
"I'm sorry, I left you," said Jack, "did you worry?
We're off on our travels, come Barney, let's hurry!"

Pauline Travers is passionate about writing poems and the performance of poetry, especially for young children. She teaches verse speaking to help children understand their voices, to improve their diction and self confidence but most importantly, to instil a love of poetry. Pauline's pupils have been successfully performing her poetry in various competitions and they have been thrilled to win many accolades with such vibrant work.

Pauline is married to Jon and they have two grown up children. They live in Cheltenham, Gloucestershire.

For further details about Pauline Travers as a visiting author please contact her via e-mail at paulinetraversat23@aol.com.

Elaine Nipper has enjoyed drawing since she was a child and has been illustrating professionally for several years. She is married to Chris and lives in Surrey.